Who Was
Alexander the Great?

Who Was
Alexander the Great?

by Kathryn Waterfield and Robin Waterfield

illustrated by Andrew Thomson

Penguin Workshop

For Zoe and Vasilis Gould
Eleni and Emanuel Rouvelas—KW & RW

To Rhia—AT

PENGUIN WORKSHOP
An imprint of Penguin Random House LLC, New York

First published in the United States of America by Penguin Workshop,
an imprint of Penguin Random House LLC, New York, 2016

Visit us online at penguinrandomhouse.com.

Library of Congress Control Number: 2016011721

Printed in the United States of America

ISBN 9780448484235 (paperback)
ISBN 9780399542350 (library binding)

15 14 13 12
10 9 8 7 6 5 4 3

Contents

Who Was Alexander the Great?

Pella, capital city of the kingdom of Macedon

It is a special day for King Philip's son. His name is Alexander, and he is twelve. He is old enough now to go to the horse market with his father and the other men.

At the market a man walks up to Philip. He claims to have the best horse in the world, one fit for a king. He is an amazing horse, sleek and strong. He is black all over, except for a white mark on his forehead. The mark is shaped like the head of an ox. That is why the horse's name is Bucephalas (say: Boo-KEH-fa-las). In Greek, *Bucephalas* means *Ox-head*.

Bucephalas is a very difficult horse to ride. Even King Philip cannot mount him. So he refuses to buy the horse and turns to leave. But young Alexander insists that *he* can ride the great horse. He wants the horse for himself.

Philip and the others don't take Alexander seriously. He is too young to ride such a dangerous horse. Alexander, however, won't take no for an answer. So the king lets him try. Maybe that will teach his stubborn son a lesson!

Is Alexander going to make a fool of himself in front of his father? No! He has noticed something that his father has not. The beautiful horse is afraid of his shadow. So Alexander walks slowly up to Bucephalas. Gently, he takes hold of the lead rope. He turns the horse into the sun, stroking his neck and whispering to him. Bucephalas cannot see his shadow now. The horse calms down. Alexander springs lightly onto its back and gallops off. Everyone is amazed!

This is Alexander's first conquest. Suddenly King Philip sees his son with new eyes. He tells Alexander that he needs to find a much bigger kingdom to rule. Macedon is too small for Alexander!

King Philip is right. Riding Bucephalas, Alexander goes on to conquer the known world. He leads thousands of soldiers thousands of miles across Asia. He becomes the richest and most powerful king alive. He builds many new cities throughout his empire. He does all this in just thirteen years! No wonder he becomes known as Alexander the Great.

CHAPTER 1
The Son of His Father

Alexander was born in 356 BC in Macedon. Macedon lay to the north of ancient Greece.

AD and BC

The system used in much of the world for dating years was invented by Christian monks hundreds of years ago. To count years they used the birth year of Jesus as the starting point. That became Year One, or AD 1. (The monks spoke and wrote in Latin. In Latin *AD* stands for *Anno Domini*, or *In the year of the Lord*.)

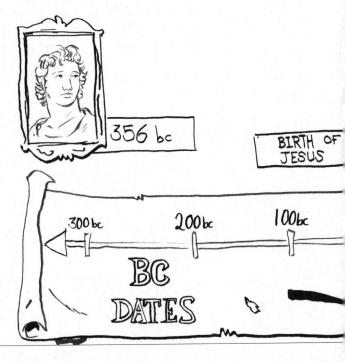

So today we are in AD times. But what about all those years *before* Jesus was born? Jesus's birth is still the starting point. The years before are counted backward. They are called years BC, or *before Christ*. Alexander the Great was born in 356 BC. This means that he was born 356 years before Jesus.

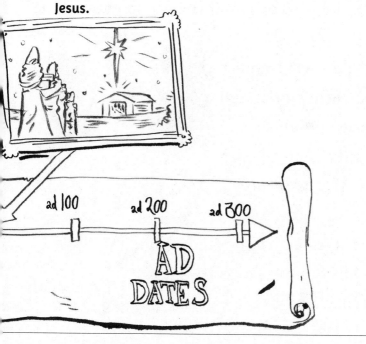

ad 100   ad 200   ad 300

AD DATES

His father, King Philip II, had seven wives. But Olympias was Philip's favorite. She gave birth to Alexander. One day, Alexander would become the next king.

Even as a baby, Alexander was famous. Amazing stories sprang up around his birth. He was supposedly descended from the famous Greek heroes Achilles and Heracles. People even said that the god Zeus was really his father, not King Philip. Zeus was the most important of the gods.

Alexander's mother liked these stories and helped spread them around the kingdom. Alexander grew up believing them, too. He felt sure that he would do great things someday.

Zeus

Ancient Macedon was a wealthy country. In the plains, crops and fruit trees grew beside wide rivers. The mountains were rich in gold and silver. Their slopes were covered with trees for timber and grazing land for sheep and goats. There were plenty of animals to hunt, too: deer, hare, birds, wild boars—and even lions!

Macedonians loved to hunt in the mountains. Hunting wild boars was extremely dangerous. But a highborn Macedonian was not considered a true man until he had killed a wild boar by himself, with just a spear.

There were other dangers in the mountains besides wild animals. Mountain tribes often raided Macedon. They stole animals, crops, and property.

In 359 BC Alexander's father became king. Philip was a great general as well as a great ruler. He wanted his people to live in safety. He made his army faster and stronger than any other.

Philip's new army beat back the enemy tribes. And he allowed Alexander, at age sixteen, to lead troops against mountain men called the Maedi. At this young age, Alexander won his first victory!

He built a town in the land of the conquered tribe. He named it Alexandropolis after himself. (In Greek, *polis* means *town*.) This was the first of many Alexander-towns.

For the first time, Macedon was peaceful and safe. But that wasn't enough for a king like Philip. He wanted Macedon to be the greatest kingdom in the world. He decided to conquer the Greeks, his neighbors to the south.

The people of Greece and Macedon were a lot alike. They worshipped the same gods. They spoke similar languages. They even looked and dressed alike. In a way, they were like cousins.

But the Greeks didn't usually have kings. Most ancient Greek states had leaders chosen by the citizens. The Greeks looked down on the Macedonians and other people who were ruled by kings. They didn't believe that Philip's army could beat their army of free men. But in 338 BC Philip did just that. The Greeks became his subjects.

What an exciting time for Alexander, the son of the king. Alexander wanted to be a great king like Philip—or even greater. He respected his father very much. But every time Philip captured a town or won a battle, Alexander complained. He said that his father wasn't leaving anything for him to conquer.

How wrong he was!

Greek and Macedonian Clothes

In the time of Alexander, men, women, and children wore similar clothes. They wore a tunic called a *khiton* (say: KIE-ton) and often, on top, a longer robe called a *himation* (say: him-AT-ieeh-on). Both were just pieces of cloth, usually wool, that wrapped around a person's body. They were fastened with big pins at the shoulders and a belt at the waist. Men and children wore their tunics shorter than women did. Women covered up completely when they went out in public. They even veiled their faces with a hood. On their feet, people usually wore leather sandals.

CHAPTER 2
A Prince's Life

Alexander always stood out from the crowd. He wasn't tall, but he was strong and handsome. His wavy hair was lighter than most Macedonians'. He brushed it back so that it looked as if the wind had blown his hair that way while he was riding Bucephalas! Most men in those days had beards, but not Alexander.

People were attracted by Alexander's good looks. But they also knew they had to be careful around him. His eyes showed his iron will. He had a quick temper. People didn't always like him. They admired him and feared him.

Alexander grew up in the royal court in Macedon. King Philip made sure the young prince had a fine education. When Alexander was young, his father found private teachers for him. He was taught to read, write, and do math. He learned to sing and play the lyre—an instrument like a small harp. He was trained in riding and hunting, and he learned to wrestle and fight with weapons. He was a very good student.

But being very good wasn't enough for Alexander. He wanted to be the best in everything.

Alexander never lost his love of books. In later life he slept with two things under his pillow: Homer's poetry and a dagger.

Homer

Around 700 BC, a man called Homer is believed to have written two long poems in Greek. They are called *The Iliad* and *The Odyssey*. They were the first books written in Europe. They are part history and part legend. *The Iliad* tells the story of the Greek war against the city of Troy in Asia. This war happened a long time before Alexander lived, around 1200 BC. *The Odyssey* is about the adventures of a Greek hero called Odysseus. He battles monsters and magic for ten years on his journey home from the Trojan War.

Girls were not usually taught to read. But all boys with schooling read *The Iliad* and *The Odyssey*.

Aristotle

Most boys finished school by the age of twelve. Not Alexander. Philip chose Aristotle, the wisest man in all Greece, to continue teaching his son.

Some years earlier, Philip had destroyed Aristotle's hometown in a war. Although Philip offered Aristotle a lot of money to tutor Alexander, he refused. He would accept the job only if Philip rebuilt his hometown and allowed its citizens to come back. Philip agreed, and Aristotle became Alexander's teacher.

Alexander was not Aristotle's only pupil. King Philip made Aristotle the head of a school of noble young men. They studied subjects such as philosophy, medicine, and science. Some of the boys there became Alexander's friends for life. His best friend was a tall, good-looking boy called Hephaestion (say: Heh-FIE-stee-on). Meanwhile, Philip was planning to fight the Persians. About a hundred fifty years before, the Persians had invaded Greece. Philip wanted to punish the Persians for these past attacks.

Hephaestion

At the time, the Persians had the greatest empire in the world. It reached all the way from the Mediterranean Sea to the Indian Ocean. There were many Greek cities in the Persian Empire. Philip promised to

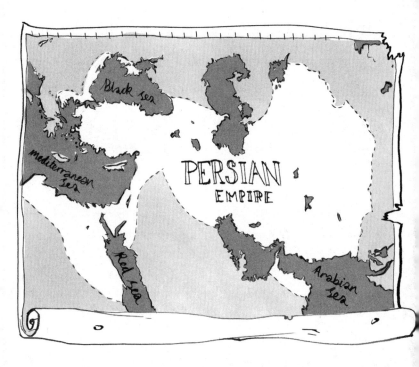

free those Greeks from Persian rule.

Whoever defeated the Persians would be the greatest king in the world. That was what Philip wanted more than anything. So did Alexander. They were confident about winning, even though the Persian army was huge. They thought that one Macedonian soldier was worth ten Persians. And the Macedonians did have better weapons.

Before King Philip went to war, he had an important duty at home. He had to celebrate the wedding of his daughter. She was marrying the ruler of a nearby kingdom.

After the wedding, there was a grand parade.

The bride and her new husband were followed by Philip and the royal family. The highest nobles of the land came next. Everyone was dressed in their finest clothes. Crowds lined the roads to see the wedding party pass by.

On this happy day Philip was not worrying about enemies. He had only two guards with him. But one of them secretly hated Philip. In the middle of the parade, he drew his dagger and stabbed the king to death!

A happy occasion suddenly turned into a murder scene. With his father dead, Alexander was now king. No one expected this to happen so soon, or in such a terrible way. But Philip had trained his son well. Alexander was ready to take power. The adventure of his life was about to begin.

King Philip's Tomb

Archeologists dig up ancient places to learn about the past. In 1977, a Greek archeologist was working in northern Greece. He decided to dig into a low hill. He thought it might be a mound built over some important graves. He was right. He discovered the tombs of the kings and queens of ancient Macedon! There were wonderful wall paintings;

there were lots of beautiful objects in gold and silver, bronze and ivory. But there was something even more exciting. One of the skeletons in the tombs had lost an eye. King Philip had lost an eye in a battle. Could this be the body of King Philip? Many scientists think so.

CHAPTER 3
The Adventure Begins

Alexander was only twenty when his father was killed in 336 BC. Now he was King Alexander III of Macedon. He longed to carry out his father's plan to fight the Persians.

Before his death, Philip had sent a small army over to Asia Minor (modern-day Turkey). In command was his best general. His name was Parmenion (say: Par-MEN-ee-on). In the spring of 334 BC, Alexander crossed the sea to join Parmenion.

Parmenion

The young king came with a much larger army. The two armies together would fight the Persians.

As his fleet approached the Asian coast, Alexander threw his spear into the sand. He was the first to jump onto the shore. With a shout he claimed the Persian Empire for himself.

Arms and Armor

Soldiers rarely wore uniforms in ancient armies. They often had to buy their own weapons and armor. Macedonian foot soldiers each wore a helmet and a breastplate made from metal, leather, or layers of pressed linen. Leather skirts protected the soldiers' thighs. They carried small shields and long, heavy spears. They fought in a solid group called a phalanx.

A Macedonian phalanx was very difficult to attack, because enemy soldiers could not get past the fence of long spears. Other foot soldiers had little or no armor. They fought with bows and arrows, slings or javelins. A soldier on horseback wore armor from head to foot. His weapons were the sword and javelin. His job was to try to break up the enemy phalanx.

Alexander and his army landed near Troy. He chose this spot because Troy was the scene of the first victory of Europeans against men of Asia. Alexander was connecting himself to the Greek heroes of Homer's *Iliad*.

Soon Alexander's army met the Persian army near Troy, on the banks of the Granicus River. As usual, Alexander led the first charge. His soldiers loved him for his bravery. But in his shining armor and plumed helmet he was easy for the enemy to spot.

It was a fierce battle, and Alexander very nearly lost his life. A blow to his head broke his helmet. As Alexander fought his assailant, a second Persian soldier had his ax raised for the final blow. But a Macedonian called Clitus rode forward just in time. He ran the Persian through with his spear and saved Alexander's life.

Finally the Persians broke and ran. The first battle was a complete victory for Alexander. But it was only the beginning. Persia was not his. Not yet.

Alexander spent the next few months conquering the rest of Asia Minor. Sometimes a city resisted him, and he had to fight to take it. At other times, cities opened their gates and welcomed him as their new king. Then, in the spring of 333 BC, he led his army southeast toward Syria. The Persian king, Darius III, was waiting there with a huge army of one hundred thousand soldiers. Alexander and Parmenion had forty thousand.

Darius III

The Gordian Knot

On the way to Syria, Alexander passed through a town called Gordium. The town was famous for a prophecy. (A *prophecy* tells what will happen in the future.) Next to the temple of Zeus there was an ancient wagon. The yoke of the wagon was joined to the shaft with strips of leather tied into a knot. The prophecy said that whoever undid the knot would rule all Asia. Although many had tried, no one could untie it. Then along came Alexander. He raised his sword and with one stroke cut through the knot. The prophecy had been fulfilled, Alexander-style!

Alexander and his army marched southeast for many weeks. The two armies met near a town called Issus. The battle ended with another victory for Alexander. He was an even greater general than his father. In fact, historians today regard Alexander as one of the greatest generals ever.

The Persian king was very rich. Many of his cities held great treasure. After the battle at Issus, Alexander seized Damascus. The treasury there held the king's gold, jewels, and other valuables. Thousands of pack animals were needed to carry it all back to Alexander's camp.

Alexander also captured Darius's mother, wife, and daughters. One day he and his friends went to visit the women. Alexander wanted to make sure they were being treated well. The women froze in fear when they saw the men enter the tent. What was going to happen? Were they going to die?

One of the men was taller and more handsome than the rest. The women supposed that must be the king! Darius's mother bowed down before him. But it wasn't the king. It was Hephaestion! All Alexander did was smile and say, "You're not wrong. This man, too, is Alexander." He was showing how close he felt to Hephaestion.

He did not return the women to Darius, but he did not hurt them. They were royal ladies, and he treated them with respect.

Darius was frightened. He offered Alexander a fortune for the return of his family. He also tried to bargain for peace. But Alexander was now sure that the Persian Empire could be his. Only a few steps were left on the path to the Persian throne.

Chapter 4
Alexander in Egypt

Alexander and his army began marching toward Egypt. This country was also part of the Persian Empire. City after city on the way to Egypt surrendered to him. They didn't put up a fight. The first to resist was Tyre, a city in what is today Lebanon. The people of Tyre thought

they were safe. Their city was on an island, about quarter of a mile from the coast. How could Alexander attack the island? There was no beach for a ship to land. And the harbors were well defended.

Alexander came up with a clever plan. For

months he made his men dump tons of stones into the sea between the coast and Tyre. Then they poured earth on top of the stones and made it level. What were they doing? They were building a road through the water . . . all the way to Tyre! And ever since then Tyre has been joined to the mainland.

Alexander brought siege engines up to the walls of Tyre. Some were catapults, like giant slingshots used to hurl huge stones. Some were giant crossbows. Others were towers so that soldiers could shoot down at the walls of Tyre. He even put one tower on a ship to attack the

city from the sea as well. He had battering rams to smash the city gates and break holes in the walls. The people inside Tyre fought back, and threw down rocks and burning-hot sand on the attackers. That didn't stop Alexander's men. In the end they broke through. The city was destroyed.

Alexander had sent a clear message: *Do not dare to resist me!* And so he continued down the coast toward Egypt.

The Egyptians were proud of their long history. For many centuries, they had been ruled by kings called pharaohs. They were unhappy under Persian rule. So the Egyptians welcomed Alexander's arrival in the fall of 332 BC. They chose to be part of Alexander's new empire. Alexander became their new pharaoh.

Alexander made plans to build a new capital city for Egypt. He did this to show that Egypt was his. He called it Alexandria—another Alexander-town! It became one of the most important cities in the world at that time. It is still there, on the north coast of Egypt.

Modern-day Alexandria

Alexandria

One part of the city of Alexandria was designated for Greeks and Macedonians. Another was for Egyptians, and then everyone else (mainly Jews) lived in the third part. The city was for many centuries a center for trade. The most splendid part was where the Greeks lived. It was right next to the harbor. Ships sailing into the harbor were greeted by some of the most magnificent buildings in the world.

Close to the royal palace was the great lighthouse. It was one of the Seven Wonders of the World. There were marble temples filled with beautiful statues of the gods and of Alexander.

One of the most famous buildings was the Museum. *Museum* means *temple of the Muses*, who were the goddesses of the arts and sciences. People came there to study and work together. The Museum of Alexandria held the world's first library. The priests there tried to collect every book that had ever been written in Greek—and every important book in other languages, too. The museum was often damaged by fire and was finally destroyed in AD 640, almost a thousand years after it was built. The lighthouse lasted even longer. Its ruins were pulled down in the fifteenth century.

Deep in the Egyptian desert, there was an oasis town called Siwah. (An *oasis* is a place in the desert where there is freshwater.) Siwah had a very famous temple. People went there to ask the god Ammon questions, and he answered them through the mouths of the priests.

Alexander crossed the desert to visit this temple. To him, Ammon was the same as the Greek god Zeus. People always said that Zeus was Alexander's father. Alexander wanted to find out for sure. That was his question for the god.

Ammon

The god's answer was a secret. But after his visit to Siwah, Alexander called himself the son of Zeus. Ammon must have given him the answer he wanted. Now Alexander expected others to recognize him as a god, too.

CHAPTER 5
Showdown!

In the spring of 331 BC, Alexander left Egypt. It was time for the final showdown with Darius. Asia Minor now belonged to Alexander. So did Syria and Egypt. But there was still the rest of the Persian Empire, which stretched all the way to where Pakistan is today. The Persian king was waiting for Alexander in the country that is now Iraq. His army was camped near a village called Gaugamela (say: Gow-ga-MAY-la).

Alexander reached Gaugamela late in September. It had been a long march. He set up camp in some low hills and let his men rest for several days.

From his camp, Alexander could see the Persian army. Darius had chosen a smart spot for a battle.

There were hills on one side of the Persians and a river on the other side. That meant that Alexander's men could not get behind them. They could not attack them from the rear or the front. Alexander knew he had only one hope. The Persians had to make a mistake during the battle.

Alexander's generals advised him to attack during the night. But Alexander refused. He said that he was not a thief. He wouldn't steal victory. Darius, however, was expecting a night attack. He kept his men awake. By morning, Alexander's men were rested and the Persians were very tired. That was when Alexander led his army down from the hills. The two armies met on a great plain.

Darius sent his war chariots forward. These chariots had long, sharp blades sticking out of their wheels. Their job was to break up the Macedonian lines. But Alexander's bowmen shot down the charioteers. Few of the chariots even reached the Macedonian lines.

Then on both sides the foot soldiers and horsemen charged forward. The battle began. Unfortunately, on the left, Parmenion's men were soon in bad trouble. Parmenion expected Alexander to send help, but Alexander stuck to his plan. A great general does not act in haste. He was waiting for his chance—waiting for the Persians to make a mistake.

Seeing that Parmenion was in trouble, more and more Persians raced over to attack him and his men. The Persians could taste victory. But they had made a mistake. There were not enough men in their center now.

This was Alexander's chance. He spurred

on Bucephalas and led his cavalry in a charge through the center. He rode straight for Darius. Terrified, Darius turned and fled in his chariot.

When Darius's men saw their king fleeing, they got scared as well. Frightened men fight badly.

Before long it was all over. The Persians scattered. Alexander's men hunted them down in the hills and killed thousands.

Alexander rode after Darius. But the Persian king was too far ahead. Alexander couldn't catch him. Not this time.

On his return to Gaugamela, Alexander went to the hospital tent. He wanted to visit the wounded men. He thanked each man for his bravery. He even helped the doctors. Aristotle had taught Alexander some medicine, so he knew what to do. His soldiers loved him for caring for them.

Darius was still free, but Alexander had won a great victory. Now there was only the far east of the Persian Empire to capture. He had all the rest. He was now the king of Asia. He had defeated the greatest empire in the world. He had made his father's dream come true.

After the battle, Alexander marched south. All the great cities of the Persian Empire surrendered to him. Babylon was his; Susa was his. Even Persepolis, the main Persian city, did not resist. Each of these cities had great riches. It all belonged to Alexander now.

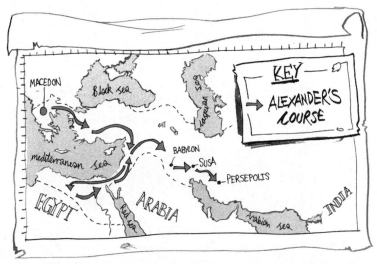

Alexander stayed in Persepolis for the winter of 331–330 BC. In the spring, he prepared to leave. He had unfinished business. He had to capture or kill Darius.

Alexander gave a great farewell feast in Persepolis. One of the women there was from the Greek city of Athens. Many years earlier, the Persians had burned Athens to the ground. Alexander had promised to punish them for that. The woman said that Alexander should keep his promise. He should burn down the great palace of Persepolis.

Alexander agreed. Everything valuable had already been removed. Alexander and the guests grabbed torches and set out for the palace. It was mostly made of wood and caught fire easily. Before long, one of the greatest buildings of the ancient world lay in ruins.

In the twentieth century archeologists dug at the ruins of the palace. After more than two thousand years, they found proof of the fire. There was still a deep layer of ash from the cedar trees used to build the palace.

CHAPTER 6
King of Persia

Darius had fled to Ecbatana. It was the only great city of the Persian Empire that was not in Alexander's hands.

In the early summer of 330 BC, Alexander marched from Persepolis to Ecbatana. What did Darius do? He fled farther east. He decided to gather an army in what is now Afghanistan. He would make his last stand there, among the green valleys and snowy mountains.

Alexander did not give up the chase. The closer he got to Darius, the more frightened the Persians became. In the end, the Persians killed their king. That was often the ancient Persian way with kings who failed at war. His cousin made himself king instead, but Alexander soon hunted him down and killed him.

It took Alexander more than two years to conquer Afghanistan. Afterward, many of his men expected to go home. Alexander had taken over the Persian Empire. Wasn't that what he came for? The job was finished. The men grumbled, but Alexander made them keep going. He wanted to conquer more lands. He wanted to be the greatest conqueror in the world.

Some of Alexander's junior officers plotted to murder him. The son of Parmenion heard about the plot. His name was Philotas (say: Fil-OAT-as). He didn't think the officers were serious, so he said nothing to Alexander.

That was a mistake. Alexander found out about the plot. He also found out that Philotas knew about it. Why had Philotas said nothing? Alexander was convinced that Philotas must be one of the plotters.

The young man was tortured and killed. After that, Alexander believed he could not trust Parmenion, either.

Philotas

He had the old general killed as well. Most of Alexander's senior officers thought that he was right to do this. But the ordinary soldiers didn't understand. They disapproved.

Why were some of Alexander's men turning against him? Maybe it was because Alexander was starting to act like a Persian king. Alexander's men looked down on the Persians. But Alexander seemed to like them. He often dressed like a Persian king. Alexander even had Persian friends in his court now.

The Great King of Persia

All the riches of the Persian Empire once belonged to Darius. Like all Persian kings, he wore his long hair oiled and curled. He had a very stiff beard. He dressed in only the finest clothes, made of silk and woven with gold thread. Persians wore trousers, unlike Macedonians or Greeks. But over his trousers the king wore a magnificent robe. Jeweled rings glittered on his fingers. He wore a crown and held a golden scepter in his right hand. He sat on a carved golden throne. Ordinary people could not speak to him directly. A message was given to one of the king's friends, and he passed it on.

In every way the Persian king was special. The Persians believed he had been chosen by their gods. The king was almost a god himself. But he couldn't rule such a big empire alone. The empire was divided into twenty countries. Each country was called a satrapy and was ruled by a satrap.

Satraps were like lesser kings to the Great King. That is why every Persian king was called the King of Kings.

Alexander behaved like this for a reason. He was the head of a huge empire. To rule it, he needed the help of Persians as well as Macedonians. He had to be a king for both Macedonians and for Persians— and even a pharaoh for Egyptians. Not all his men understood this. But Alexander was the king.

He did not let his men tell him how to behave.

Now Alexander sat on a golden throne. His huge tent had gold everywhere. Even the tent poles were golden. Inside the tent, he was surrounded by Persian and Macedonian guards. Outside, his tent was guarded by elephants dressed for battle.

Persians bowed down before Alexander. They had always bowed before the Great King. Alexander now ordered *all* his men to bow before him. But Greeks and Macedonians had only bowed before their gods. Some of them refused to obey. To them, it seemed that all this wealth and power had changed Alexander.

In the old days, any Macedonian nobleman could speak his mind to his king. Now it became dangerous to do that. Alexander did not want to hear that he was wrong about anything.

One night Alexander threw a party for the senior Macedonian officers. His friend Clitus came. He was the man who had saved the king's life at the Granicus River. A lot of wine was drunk. Alexander began to brag about his successes. This did not go down well with Clitus.

Clitus said that Alexander was too high-and-mighty. He said that Alexander was the son of Philip, not of Zeus. He was a man, not a god. The two men began to shout at each other. Some of the guests hurried Clitus out of the tent, but he came back. In a rage, Alexander grabbed a spear from a guard and killed his friend.

Afterward the king was filled with guilt and grief. He shut himself in his tent. He would see no one. He refused to eat or drink. This went on for three days.

Alexander's officers were worried. They sent a message to the king. They said that the king was right and Clitus was wrong. Still Alexander stayed in his tent. Finally his friends persuaded Alexander to start eating. Everyone hoped that now all would be well. But the men wondered: Would Alexander be his old self again?

Alexander did seem more at peace with himself. In the spring of 327 BC, before leaving Afghanistan, he got married. His bride was the daughter of an Afghan chief. Her name was Rhoxana. It means *Little Star*.

Rhoxana was Alexander's first wife. If she had a son, he would be the next king. But she wasn't Macedonian. So the next king would have mixed blood. This, too, made many of his men unhappy.

Trouble was brewing for King Alexander.

CHAPTER 7
To the Edge of the World

All of the Persian Empire belonged now to Alexander. What land did he want to conquer next? India.

In Alexander's time, no one had any idea how far India went. People said that it was at the very edge of the world. Alexander wanted to find out.

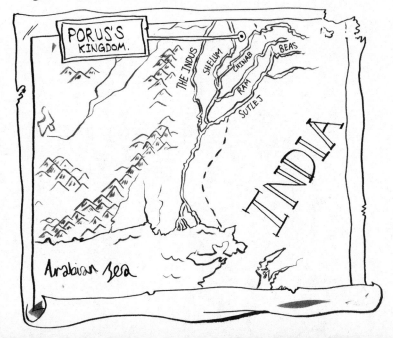

Greeks and Macedonians believed that the world was surrounded by a huge river. This river, called Ocean, flowed all the way around the edge of the world. No one had ever seen it. Only heroes and gods had ever visited it. Alexander wanted to reach Ocean. That would prove he was more than human.

Many of the peoples of India did not want to be ruled by Alexander. The first to resist was Porus. He was king of a rich land. King Porus was seven feet tall, and he rode a mighty war elephant.

Alexander set up camp across the river from Porus and his army. It was late in the spring of 326 BC. Porus knew that the summer rains were starting. Soon the river would be too deep and fast for Alexander to cross.

But, as always, Alexander had a plan. He divided his army into four groups along the riverbank. Porus could see them. He thought his army had only to guard against four crossings. But Alexander was tricking Porus. He secretly took a fifth group up the river. He had ships and rafts hidden behind an island there. Under the cover of a rainstorm, Alexander and his men crossed safely to the other side.

War Elephants

Elephants are smart. They are also brave. We know from seeing circus elephants do tricks that they can be trained. Indians began training them for war around 1000 BC. From India, the Persians learned to use elephants in battle. They were enormous and very frightening. They were trained to charge the enemy and crush soldiers with their feet and tusks. Each elephant had a trainer. He was called a mahout. He sat on the elephant's neck, just behind the ears, and drove it. Soldiers also rode on the back of each elephant, in a wooden tower called a howdah or castle. From there they fired arrows down at the enemy. The first time Macedonians met war elephants was at Gaugamela in 331 BC. In that battle Alexander captured fifteen of the creatures. From then on, he used them, too.

The two armies met on the southern bank of the river. Although Porus had fewer men than Alexander, he had as many as two hundred elephants. But it didn't matter. With their long spears Alexander's men could kill the elephants' riders. They also wounded the elephants. In the end, Porus's elephants did little harm.

Meanwhile, Alexander's other forces crossed the river. Porus's army was surrounded. The battle lasted only a few hours. Porus was defeated. Very few of the Indians escaped.

Porus fought bravely to the end. He gave in only after being badly wounded. Alexander respected the Indian king. He needed an ally like him. He made Porus his friend and let him remain king. Of course, Porus understood that he was just a king. Alexander was the King of Kings.

Sadly, Bucephalas died after the battle. He had carried Alexander thousands of miles.

But by this time he was old. Alexander rarely rode him. Still, Alexander was heartbroken. He held a special funeral for Bucephalas. Afterward, Alexander built a town in Porus's kingdom. He named it Bucephalia, after his beloved horse. No trace has ever been found of this town.

Next Alexander crossed the Chenab and Ravi rivers. No one could stop him. He easily won every battle. There was only one force he was no match for—the weather.

The summer monsoon had begun. The monsoon is heavy rain lasting for about three months. Day after day, the rain fell without stopping. For men on the march, there was nothing worse. They were never dry. They were caked in mud. They fell ill. Their shoes rotted. Their weapons rusted. And their spirits sank.

Many of Alexander's men were angry at being so far from home. They had fought long and hard for their king. They had conquered the Persian Empire. That was enough.

Not for Alexander. He was set on reaching Ocean and the edge of the world. The army marched for more than seventy days in the monsoon. When they came to the Beas River, Alexander ordered his men to cross. There were more tribes to conquer. He wanted to reach the River Ocean.

The men refused to carry on. Alexander was furious. He sulked in his tent for days. But even his priests told him that the gods were against him.

Could it be true that the gods were against him, as well as his men? That was too much even for Alexander to risk. He agreed to turn back. But the army had to take a long route. There was more Alexander wanted to see and do. The adventure would continue . . . for a while.

CHAPTER 8
The Desert March

Alexander and his men set out for the great city of Babylon, which he planned to make the capital of his empire. Alexander's men built ships and sailed down the Jhelum River toward the

coast. As usual, towns and tribes surrendered or were defeated on the way.

In a battle with the Mallian tribe, once again Alexander led the attack. He was the first to climb a ladder to the top of a city wall. Enemy arrows, spears, and stones flew thick and fast around him.

His men quickly followed. They were eager to rescue their king. But too many were rushing up the ladders. The ladders broke. There Alexander was, on top of the wall, with only very few soldiers beside him!

Alexander leaped down into the city streets. Soon he was surrounded by Mallian soldiers. An arrow struck Alexander in the chest and he fell to the ground.

His death seemed certain. But somehow his few companions beat the enemy back. At last the Macedonian army broke in. Furious at the wounding of their king, they killed everyone.

Alexander was carried back to camp on a shield. He was more dead than alive. What would happen if the king died? The Macedonians felt it would be impossible to get home without their great leader's skill and luck.

The arrow was carefully removed from his chest. It had pierced a lung. Alexander lost a lot of blood. For days he was too weak to leave his tent. But he left the tent open. His men needed to see him alive. Slowly the king got better.

The army reached the coast in July 325 BC.

There they prepared for the journey west. Many more ships were built. The army was divided into three parts. One part would sail along the coast. Another would march well inland. Alexander would take the third part through the desert. They would all meet again on the Persian Gulf.

Why did Alexander choose the desert route? There would be little water. Food would be hard to find. Perhaps he didn't know how bad it would be. Or perhaps he wanted to do something extra dangerous. Hundreds of Alexander's men died on the desert march. They died from thirst and hunger. They were so hungry, they ate their pack animals. But then there was nothing to eat. Everyone suffered, and Alexander suffered with them.

Once, one of the soldiers found some water. It was just enough to fill the bottom of his helmet. The man took the water to his king. But Alexander wouldn't drink unless his men could drink, too. And there was only a little water. Alexander poured it on the ground for the gods. His men cheered and carried on.

It took two months to reach the end of the desert. At last there was plenty to eat and drink. Alexander let the men get drunk on wine as they marched.

He rode on his chariot dressed as the god of wine.

Finally they reached Susa. Alexander held a great wedding there. More than ninety noble Macedonians were married to noble eastern women. Alexander himself married Darius's daughter and the daughter of the king before Darius. Hephaestion married another daughter of Darius. He and Alexander were now almost brothers. Alexander gave generous gifts to all the new bridegrooms.

The wedding party went on for several days. It should have been a happy time. But some of the soldiers were unhappy. They didn't want eastern wives. They missed King Philip, Alexander's father. *He* had been a true Macedonian.

CHAPTER 9
Death in Babylon

Alexander left Susa in the spring of 324 BC. By summer he had arrived at Ecbatana, in the mountains. The weather was cooler there. Persian kings often stayed there in the summer.

Countries and cities and tribes from all over Asia sent men to Ecbatana. Everyone wanted to greet the new king. Everyone wanted to be his friend.

Alexander held a great feast. In the middle of it, Hephaestion fell ill. A few days later he died. Hephaestion had been Alexander's one true friend. For the first time he felt completely alone. No one could console him. Yet even in his grief, he was determined to reach Babylon.

The army left Ecbatana in the spring of 323 BC. They made a grand entry into Babylon. The Babylonian priests warned the king *not* to enter the city. They had read in the stars that something bad would happen to him.

Alexander ignored them. He made the great palace of Babylon his home. Rhoxana was with him, and all the friends who made up his court.

Rhoxana was expecting a baby. If it were a boy, he would be king after Alexander.

Alexander had begun his great adventure as king of Macedon and Greece. When he crossed to Asia and defeated Darius he added the Persian Empire and Egypt to his kingdom. He even ruled some of India, at the very edge of the known world.

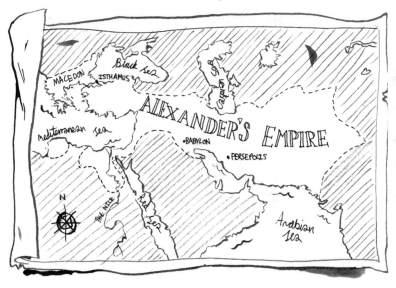

In all, by 323 BC Alexander's empire covered two million square miles! But, being Alexander, nothing was ever enough.

In Babylon, Alexander planned more conquests. He wanted to conquer Arabia next. And after Arabia, he planned to march west from Egypt to conquer all North Africa. Then he'd move on to Spain and Italy. If his men were tired, he would send them home and find fresh troops to lead in battle.

By the spring, a huge fleet of ships had gathered at Babylon. Satraps brought troops from all over Alexander's empire. The army was bigger than ever. Everything was ready for the attack on Arabia.

Alexander ordered a celebration. His officers were glad because Alexander seemed to be getting over Hephaestion's death. But others were worried. Had the priests read the stars correctly? Was something bad awaiting Alexander?

Yes!

During the party, Alexander suddenly fell sick. He became weak and feverish. He stayed in bed all the next day. Then he tried going about his business. But the fever grew worse. Soon Alexander was so weak that he couldn't even talk.

The king's generals were very worried. If he died, who would be king? Rhoxana's baby wasn't born yet. And it might be a girl. Girls could not rule.

Alexander grew worse. He was barely breathing. Hundreds of his men lined up for a last look at their dying king. Quietly they filed past his bed. Some whispered prayers. Others were crying. They paid respects to the king they loved and feared.

Alexander died on June 10, 323 BC. He was not quite thirty-three years old.

Many people believed he had been killed. Had he been given poison at the party? Rumors of murder spread around the empire. No one was sure how the king had died. Some historians believe Alexander never really recovered from the arrow that struck his lung. But to this day, no one is certain what caused his death.

At Babylon, Alexander's body was preserved. Special chemicals and herbs kept it from decaying.

Many years later, visitors to Alexander's tomb said that he still looked young and handsome!

A fabulous wagon was built to carry Alexander's body back to Macedon. It took two years to build. The wagon looked like a small temple on wheels. Everything was gold with scenes carved on all four sides. Golden nets hung down to shade the coffin but allow people to see inside.

Crowds lined the roads from Babylon to see the wagon pulled by sixty-four mules, each with a jeweled harness. People waited for just a glimpse of the great king.

Alexander never returned home, however. One of his generals stole the wagon and took it to Egypt. This general was named Ptolemy. Ptolemy was going to be the king of Egypt. He believed that Alexander should be buried in Alexandria. It was the greatest Alexander-town. He felt

Ptolemy

Alexander belonged there. A tomb was built for him that people visited for many centuries. However, no one knows exactly where it is today.

Alexander was "great" because he did so much, so quickly. Thanks to his skills as a war leader, he led an army in victory to the very ends of the known world. He brought Europeans deep into Asia. Thousands of them stayed and made their homes there. They brought their language, religion, and art to places where they had never been seen or heard before. Alexander changed the world forever.

Alexander had a dream. He dreamed that his empire would be ruled by men from the West *and* men from the East. He believed that East and West need not always fight. Perhaps they could live together in peace. This, too, is why Alexander was great.

What happened to Alexander's empire? Almost as soon as the king died, his generals began to fight for power. None managed to win the whole empire for himself. At the end of many years of war, three leaders became kings of parts of Alexander's empire. Ptolemy, the man who stole Alexander's body, became the king of Egypt, and two others took other parts of the empire for themselves. None of them ever matched Alexander's achievements.

Only Alexander won the right to be called "the Great."

ine of Alexander the Great's Life

- Reign of Philip II, father of Alexander
- Birth of Alexander in July
- Aristotle becomes Alexander's tutor
- Alexander builds Alexandropolis
- Philip conquers the Greeks
- Murder of Philip
- Alexander becomes king of Macedon
- Alexander crosses from Europe to Asia
- Battle of Granicus River
- Alexander cuts Gordian knot
- Battle of Issus
- Capture of Damascus
- Egypt surrenders to Alexander
- Building of Alexandria begins
- Battle of Gaugamela
- Burning of palace at Persepolis
- Darius III killed
- Deaths of Philotas and Parmenion
- Conquest of Afghanistan
- Alexander marries Rhoxana
- Alexander in India
- Mass wedding at Susa
- Death of Hephaestion
- Alexander dies in Babylon

Timeline of the World

550–330 BC	Persian Achaemenid Empire
490–480 BC	Persians invade Greece and sack Athens
475–221 BC	Era of the Warring States in China
437–272 BC	Romans gain control of Italy
404–343 BC	Egypt independent of Persian rule
c. 400 BC	The Mahābhārata, the world's longest poem, takes shape in India
c. 390 BC	Invention in Greece of catapult as weapon of war
387 BC	Sack of Rome by Celts
383 BC	Second Buddhist Council, in India
c. 371-289 BC	Mencius, Chinese philosopher
c. 360 BC	Olmec Great Pyramid built in Mexico
c. 347 BC	Death of Plato, Greek philosopher
343-332 BC	Egypt again under Persian rule
c. 330 BC	The Greek explorer, Pytheas of Massilia, reaches Britain
c. 330-320 BC	Euclid, Greek mathematician, writes his Elements
322 BC	Death of Aristotle, Greek philosopher
321-185 BC	Mauryan Empire in India
312 BC	Construction of the first aqueduct begun in Rome
	Construction of Appian Way begun in Rome
c. 300 BC	End of Jomon culture in Japan
c. 270 BC	Aristarchus of Samos proposes that the sun is at the center of the universe

Bibliography

Adams, Winthrop Lindsay. *Alexander the Great: Legacy of a Conqueror.* New York: Pearson/Longman, 2006.

Heckel, Waldemar, and Lawrence Tritle, eds. *Alexander the Great: A New History.* Malden, MA: Blackwell, 2009.

Heckel, Waldemar, and J.C. Yardley, eds. *Alexander the Great. Historical Sources in Translation.* Malden, MA: Blackwell, 2003.

Renault, Mary. *The Nature of Alexander.* London: Lane, 1975.

Worthington, Ian. *Alexander the Great: A Reader.* Second edition. New York: Routledge, 2012.